HEALING FROM A BREAKUP CHRIST'S WAY

HEALING
From a
BREAK UP
CHRIST'S
Way

Finding freedom, peace, and healing from relationship
strongholds through God's word and spiritual expressive arts!

DEATHA S. HALL

CONTENTS

⁓ INTRODUCTION ⁓

Relationships are essential to function in the world we live in. Rather it be biological, friendships, romantic, or spiritual, God designed us to be in connection with one another. The Word of God teaches us that our most valuable relationship is with our Heavenly Father. At one period in my life, my relationship with God was of low priority. During that time, I was overwhelmed with sadness and anxiety questioning, was this all my life had to offer? I am sure many of you can identify with being distracted by the cares of this world, neglecting your spiritual life. It happens! The Holy Spirit revealed to me that placing anything or anyone above my relationship with God was a sin. Thankfully, by grace we are adopted into the Kingdom of God. We belong to God, and as His children we can come confidently before the throne of grace to obtain mercy. If you find yourself in a similar situation, now is the time to humble yourselves before God and repent. This is the choice we have as believers.

If you are not a born-again believer, I encourage you to repent of your ways and accept Jesus Christ as Lord and Savior. The Bible indicates the first step to salvation is confession. Romans 10:9-10 states, "if you declare with your mouth, "Jesus is Lord," and believe in your heart that God raised him from the dead, you will be saved. [10] For it is with your heart, that you believe and are justified, and it is with your mouth that you profess your faith and are saved."

I pray the Holy Spirit compels you to make this declaration and receive the gift of salvation. We should all come before God with a repentant heart. God honors humility, and when you come to Him with a contrite spirit, the response would be healing. Now, we have a clean slate and can delve deeper into romantic relationships. Genesis 2:18 reads, Now the Lord God said, "It is not good (beneficial) for the man to be alone; I will make him a helper [one who balances him—a counterpart who is] suitable and complementary for him". However, relationships not conducive to our walk with Christ can be detrimental to our wellbeing.

This book will take you on a journey of how I prioritized my spiritual relationship and ultimately received healing. I believe me sharing my story will strengthen the next person to seek God in overcoming their relationship strongholds. The power and application of God's word will lead to transformation, growth, and maturity.

≈ PROLOGUE: IT'S A LOVE THING ≈

Scripture: And to know the love of Christ, which passeth knowledge, that ye might be filled with all the fullness of God -Ephesians 3:19 KJV

And the light bulb goes off... As a regular churchgoer, you often hear "God loves you!" It is embedded in your head. I was born and raised in a Pentecostal church. Growing up in my generation, I attended church multiple days a week. Tuesday was choir rehearsal, Wednesday was Bible Class, Thursday was deliverance service, and Sunday was the traditional worship service. Now, this was not the typical Sunday service in which service lasted 2 hours. No, we stayed in church ALL DAY long. Sunday School, Morning worship, and afternoon service. The emphasis on the "all day" is literal. Then, there were revivals, outdoor musicals, church/ pastor anniversaries, and visits to sister churches. It was no such thing as attending church one day a week for 2 hours. Church was my life. I smile at just the thought. Do not get me wrong, these were some of the best memories from my childhood. I recall my cousins and I jumping up and down, holding on to the back of the pews as the shouting music started. We would imitate various members, dancing, falling out, sleeping, etc. This was pure bliss in our eyes. We were a small family-based church, so going to church also meant spending time with my family. It was a lot of us in the same age group. I sang in the choir, served on the usher and nurses board, directed the choir (Adult and Junior), taught Sunday School and Vacation Bible School. I considered all this foundational religion (or beginners training). I was perceived to be a good Christian girl and that was enough. I knew God, based on those religious routines; on the way I saw other members conduct themselves. As I transitioned into adulthood, I continued to follow those routines. Attending church out of habit, but I did not allow God's love to FULLY manifest in my life. I was comfortable staying behind the scenes, not drawing too much attention to myself and what I was doing.

Metaphorically speaking, church was my life. I accepted Christ at a young age, and I was saved according to Romans 10:9. There was no doubt Christ died on the cross for my sins, and I confessed He was my risen Lord and King. However, there was no intimacy with God and as a result, I was spiritually blind to His great love. Sometimes it takes a life altering situation for you to understand the depths of God's love. "You can't play with God", as the older saints would say. You must know Him for yourself. In my case, it took the turmoil of a relationship stronghold for me to fully experience intimacy with God. He heard my cries and rescued me from my despair. He comforted me with his presence and let me know He was my first love.

At times, it may be difficult for you to comprehend God's love because of your earthly examples of love. Earth's love has conditions, it is temporal and has contingencies; however, God's love is extraordinary, everlasting, and unconditional. Even in our sin when we do not love ourselves, God overshadows us with His love. God longs for intimacy with His people. He created you just to have a relationship with you. The whole purpose of Jesus dying on the cross for our sins was for humanity to be reconciled in relationship to God. He wants us to be fully satisfied in His love regardless of what is going on in our life.

Consider relationships in the natural sense. When you begin a new relationship, there is an excitement to know and learn more about your partner. This occurs by spending time together. You are eager to share more of yourself. We all have been there; some call it the honeymoon phase. We should continuously display the same eagerness in our relationship with God; there should be a hunger to be in His presence and to know more of Him. God loves us so much that He reveals Himself through the Holy Spirit. The more time we spend with God, the more His Love illuminates us. Our eyes are opened to His great love. During those intimate moments with our Heavenly Father, we will receive revelation knowledge of His word, resulting in an abundance of insight necessary to experience the Kingdom of Heaven. Jesus prayed, "Your will be done on earth, as it is in heaven." We can experience heaven on earth when we understand the depths of God's love. There are no limits, as we will be filled with the fullness of God. As you gain understanding of God's love, you want to spend more time with him. You want to please, honor, and glorify him. You will see your life elevate when you begin to love yourself the way God loves you. I once heard, "how can I love you, and you don't even love yourself?" When you spend time with God, you will start to take on His characteristics, which includes seeing yourself the way He sees you.

How does God see you?

"So God created man in his own image, in the image of God created he him; male and female created he them. And God saw everything that he had made, and, behold, it was very good…." -Genesis 1:27, 31 KJV

"For You formed my innermost parts; you knit me together in my mother's womb. I will praise thee; for I am fearfully and wonderfully made: marvelous are thy works; and that my soul knoweth right well." – Psalms 129:14 KJV

"Behold, I have graven thee upon the psalms of my hands; thy walls are continually before me." - Isaiah 49:16 KJV

But the very hairs of your head are all numbered. Fear ye not therefore, ye are of more value than many sparrows.
-Mathew 10:30-31 KJV

For thou hast made him a little lower than the angels, and hast crowned him with glory and honor. -Psalms 8:5 KJV

"I said, "You are gods; Indeed, all of you are sons of the Most High." - Psalms 82:6 AMP

"How precious also are thy thoughts unto me, O God! How great is the sum of them! If I should count them, they are more in number than the sand: when I awake, I am still with thee."
-Psalms 139:17-18 KJV

"Keep me as the apple of your eye; hide me in the shadow of your wings."- Psalms 17:8 KJV

"For I know the thoughts that I think toward you, saith the Lord, thoughts of peace, and not of evil, to give you an expected end. Then shall ye call upon me, and ye shall go and pray unto me, and I will hearken unto you. And ye shall seek me, and find me, when ye shall search for me with all your heart."- Jeremiah 29:11-13 KJV

God sees you as His perfect creation. He knows every detail about you, the good and the bad, yet he calls you valuable. He has good thoughts towards His children, which outnumber the sand in the sea. He is ALWAYS thinking of YOU! You are the focus point of His vision, and He wants good things for you.

When you know you have the greatest love of all, you begin to move differently. Your thoughts, attitudes, beliefs, and actions begin to reflect the love of God. So, I pray you allow the fresh anointing of God's love to fall upon you. I pray you begin to see yourself the way God sees you and attract the same type of earthly love!!

∿ **Exercise** ∿

"I am" are the two most powerful words you can declare because what comes after that frames your perspective as well as your reality. God is the great I AM. When God speaks, He affirms who He is and what He is about to do with "I am". Jeremiah 32:37 reads "Behold, I am the Lord, the God of all flesh: is there anything too hard for me?"

Below is a practical exercise of positive affirmations you can recite to see yourself how God sees you. Begin to develop your own "I am" confessions of who you are in Christ Jesus.

I am...
I am God's perfect creation
I am a child of God
I am God's own, I belong to Him
I have full access to God of this Universe, my Abba Father
I am fearfully and wonderfully made by God
I am important to God
I am valuable to God
I am validated by God

_____

_____

_____

_____

_____

_____

_____

_____

Meditate on God's "I am" statements

I am the Almighty God; walk before me, and be thou perfect -
Genesis 17:1 KJV

I am the Lord, who heals you - Exodus 15:26 NIV

I am Alpha and Omega, the beginning and the ending, saith
the Lord, which is, and which was, and which is to come, the
Almighty. - Revelation 1:8 KJV

I am the God Shepherd; the good Shepherd giveth his life for
the sheep. -John 10:11KJV

I am bread of life. -John 6:48 KJV

I am the resurrection, and the life: he that believeth in me,
though he were dead, yet shall he live. - John 11:25 KJV

And God said unto Moses, I AM THAT I AM: and he said,
Thus, shalt thou say unto the children of Israel. I AM hath sent
me unto you. -Exodus 3:13KJV

PART I

DEVOTION

CHAPTER ONE
～ DEVOTION IS HARD TO COME BY... ～
"Devoted but not a fool..."

After years in a committed intimate relationship, I began to question the authenticity of love from my partner. I often wondered, do the words I hear match the action I see. When contemplating our relationship, my partner voiced to me "you are a devoted woman, and you can't buy that nowadays." After my blank expression and lack of affection over his words, my partner repeated his statement. This led to my curiosity on the concept of a devoted woman. What it means and why is it so non-existent?

Devotion is described as a sense of incomparable loyalty towards one or one's cause. Devotion in the intimate sense may be described as the act of being faithful to a partner. I pondered on that definition, thinking of course I am devoted, that is what you do for someone you love and want to spend the rest of your life with.

> *It can't be love if Christ ain't in it. It's just a physical attraction, an emotional reaction. Love is a spirit, much more than a feeling. That's why I say, it can't be love if Christ ain't in it"*- Excerpt from "It Can't Be Love", Song written by my father, Gerald Hall.

That devotion became very costly. My unhealthy devotion to the wrong partner came with many sleepless nights, troubling thoughts, and overwhelming feelings of anxiety. As the years passed, intimacy became extinct. We were not spending time with one another only when it was sexually convenient. I can recall being in a relationship but experiencing extreme periods of loneliness. Infidelity, deceit, psychological abuse, and negative emotional charged behaviors defined the relationship. Sure, there were good times, but the bad outweighed those moments. The environment was completely toxic for my daughters and me. I often thought, was this the example I wanted to set for them? "Do I want my daughters to follow my footsteps in their relationships?" I am not stating this to degrade anyone's character or as we would say in the urban context "take jabs at someone", but simply describe how relationship distractions can be detrimental to our mental, physical, and spiritual well-being. Let us not forget the emotional toil it takes on our minds.

I am reminded of the times I fell asleep under the weight of anxiety and stress asking myself is this all life has to offer? Is this how love feels? I specifically recall waking up to my partner stumbling in the house in the middle of the night. My ears became sensitive to the unlocking of the doors. He would sometimes cook himself some food or shower prior to coming to bed, but it never failed that he would listen to music. It was some of the biggest R&B jams and love songs. I remember laying on my side forcing myself to stay awake knowing this was my opportunity. My chance to uncover the lies and secure solid evidence to walk away. You see, his phone was connected to the Bluetooth and when playing music on certain streaming platforms, the phone did not lock. Thus, I had unrestricted access without knowing his password. I subconsciously played the mission impossible music in my head, knowing time was of the essence. In my mind, he would fall asleep listening to music, and then I would be able to roam thru his phone. I always would find something inappropriate but ask me did I walk away. Words of wisdom: if you have to go searching, you will find something. This became an unhealthy cycle; the mental turmoil of it all. My emotions were a whirlwind, and the relationship became my primary focus, exalting or taking preeminence in my life over God. We will delve deeper into the topic of idolatry and relationship strongholds later in the book, but please understand the enemy desires to sift us as wheat. However, Jesus is praying for us in Heaven that our faith does not fail. John 10:10 states, "The thief comes only to steal and kill and destroy; I have come that they may have life and have it to the full." The enemy attempted to take my mind and kill my spirit, but God said, "not so!" "She is my chosen one!" This is how God sees us, as his own. Thanks be unto to God who always causes us to triumph!

Devotion to your partner is not ineffectual; however, there is a divine order in every good and perfect thing. Jesus taught us in Mark 12:29-31, two commandments that believers are mandated to follow:

"And Jesus answered him, the first of all the commandments is, Hear, O Israel; The Lord our God is one Lord:
30 And thou shalt love the Lord thy God with all thy heart, and with all thy soul, and with all thy mind, and with all thy strength: this is the first commandment. *31 And the second is like, namely this, Thou shalt love thy neighbor as thyself. There is none other commandment greater than these.*

Yes, in that order! First God, next yourself, and then your neighbor. Some may interpret the second commandment to mean love your neighbor before yourself. However, God revealed to me that I cannot properly love someone if I do not love myself. There is a direct correlation between love and devotion. Your love for someone measures your level of loyalty, which is why devotion exclusively to your partner without commitment to the heavenly Father is detrimental to your spirit. If the relationship is not what God ordered, then the impact is greater. How do we know if we are with the partner God designed for us? As the songwriter wrote, "it can't be love if Christ ain't in it. Love is a spirit and to love, Jesus's spirit must dwell in you." So, when examining if you are in the relationship that God predestined for you, look to Jesus who is the exact manifestation of love. The Lord gave me in a dream that my soul mate would usher me into the presence of God and my purpose in life. We would be a helpmeet for one another, encouraging each other to reach our identity in Christ. Thus, our relationships should not hinder our spiritual journey but enhance our walk with Christ.

You may be contemplating ending a relationship or trying to heal from a breakup. You may be experiencing some of the same emotions that I described earlier: loneliness; overwhelming feelings of anxiety or uncertainty about the future; troubling thoughts. In all the pain, I guarantee you there is peace and sunshine at the end of the tunnel. Just as I found balance in the Word of God and the leadership of the Holy Spirit, you will as well. God is no respecter of person. He is able to use anyone as His living vessel to accomplish His will. In life, we go through challenges so we can learn more of God and more of ourselves. What I love about God is that He never allows anyone to go thru these challenges alone. God says in Deuteronomy 31:6 "Be strong and courageous. Do not fear or be in dread of them, for it is the Lord your God who goes with you. He will not leave you or forsake you." Isaiah 41:10 instructs, "Fear thou not: for I am with thee; be you dismayed; for I am thy God; I will strengthen thee; yea, I will help thee; yea, I will uphold thee with the right hand of my righteousness. Psalms 94:14 reads, "For the Lord will not cast off his people, neither will he forsake his inheritance."

We can rest assure and stand on God's word believing all His promises are fulfilled through Christ Jesus. He is always with us. He will never abandon us. Everything we need, He is. Now unto him who is able to do exceedingly abundantly above all we can ask or think according to the power that worketh in us (Ephesians 3:20, KJV). The scripture clearly references the importance of doing the work. It took work and dedication to choose God and myself to walk in the healing that God promised us.

> Scripture: "The one who does not love has not become acquainted with God [does not and never did know Him], for God is love. [He is the originator of love, and it is an enduring attribute of His nature.]"- 1 John 4:8 AMP

CHAPTER TWO
≈ DEVOTION – CHOOSING GOD ≈
"Everything he's done to you, you've done to me." - God

The release of your feelings and emotions can be healing to the soul. This was my way to plead sincerely with my partner to change, almost as an intervention. I poured out my heart with a mental checklist of all my concerns and feelings. I felt temporary relief knowing I was able to release all those things that I allowed to fester. After my makeshift intervention, in a still yet powerful voice God whispered, "everything he's done to you, you've done to me." Rejection, lack of commitment, lack of trust, being used as a convenience …could that describe my relationship with God? Immediately, I asked God for forgiveness and cried out to the Lord. No longer was it about my feelings, but the Lord had an intervention with me. He revealed to me I was on a path of destruction. Thank God for His Holy Spirit that gracefully corrects us. As a result, I was able to take inventory of my relationship with God. Throughout the course of our spiritual journey, we will have periods of self-reflection and evaluation. I asked myself, "Where was my relationship with God?" Do I love the Lord more than anything? Where is my heart? Where do my treasures lie? What/ Who do I put my trust and hope in?

My confession:

"It saddens me to reveal that I would describe my relationship with God as lukewarm. I'm not all in. I use God at my convenience instead of making Him Lord of my life."
Journal Entry 8/2/18

My Lord, what a revelation! To confess I was having a casual relationship with my heavenly Father. When imagining a casual relationship in the natural sense, I think about benefits with no commitment. God is bestowing all these blessings upon me, while I say I appreciate Him, my actions reflect that of an ungrateful lover. I lack commitment, I do what I want without acknowledgment, I dedicate time at my convenience solely as it benefits me. Thank you, Father for your renewed mercies that extend from everlasting to everlasting. After self-evaluation, hopefully comes action to walk towards God and the path of righteousness. I want to make my Creator Lord of my life. To get to that point, I must make some difficult decisions and surrender my all to the Lord. In your relationship, you must do the same and ask yourself "where do my treasures lie?" Do you put your trust and faith in the relationship, or do you put trust and faith in God to guide the relationship? There is a difference.

RELATIONSHIP STRONGHOLDS

How does a relationship with God become as I described above "casual"? To answer that question, you must understand idol worshipping and strongholds. The Bible states, "For though we walk in the flesh, we do not war after the flesh: (For the weapons of our warfare are not carnal, but mighty through God to the pulling down of strong holds;) Casting down imaginations, and every high thing that exalteth itself against the knowledge of God, and bringing into captivity every thought to the obedience of Christ;" (2 Corinthians 10:3-5, KJV). Essentially, anything or anyone that you put more focus on then God can potentially manifest into a stronghold. Exalting or regarding something as more important than your relationship with God is ultimately making that thing or person an idol. Sometimes you must examine your actions to determine if your romantic relationship has become more important to you than your relationship with God.

〜 Exercise 〜

Sometimes you must examine your actions to determine if your romantic relationship has become more important to you than your relationship with God. Ask yourself the questions below and record your responses:

Do I spend more time worrying about the relationship, than I spend time with God?
Do I find myself making sacrifices for the sake of the relationship that hinder my spiritual development?
Do I find myself stuck?
Who do I turn to when I have difficulties in the relationship?
What do I sacrifice for the sake of the relationship?
Do I value intimacy with my partner more than I desire intimacy with God?
Is God included in the equation of the relationship?

_____

_____

_____

_____

_____

_____

_____

_____

_____

Did you find yourself answering yes to some of the questions? What have your responses indicated? Examining your actions is imperative to understanding if you have exalted your relationship above God thus making it an idol. A relationship stronghold is not something we can break free of with our carnal mind. We must take on the mind of Jesus. Thanks be unto God for His word and perfect instructions on how we are to deal with relationship strongholds.

> *Scripture: Finally, my brethren, be strong in the Lord, and in the power of his might. Put on the whole armour of God, that ye may be able to stand against the wiles of the devil. For we wrestle not against flesh and blood, but against principalities, against powers, against the rulers of the darkness of this world, against spiritual wickedness in high places. Wherefore take unto you the whole armour of God that ye may be able to withstand in the evil day, and having done all, to stand. Stand therefore, having your loins girt about with truth, and having on the breastplate of righteousness; And your feet shod with the preparation of the gospel of peace; Above all, taking the shield of faith, wherewith ye shall be able to quench all the fiery darts of the wicked. And take the helmet of salvation, and the sword of the Spirit, which is the word of God: Praying always with all prayer and supplication in the Spirit, and watching thereunto with all perseverance and supplication for all saints;"*
> *-Ephesians 6:10-18 KJV*

From this scripture, I learned relationship strongholds are strategies and schemes from the enemy to have people continuing in the path of sin. The scripture reads this is not a fight between flesh and blood, but a spiritual battle. Please understand this is a fight for your soul to steal your destiny. The enemy desires to take our mind, to distract us from our true purpose in God. We must take a stand and become soldiers for Christ. For this text, we will focus on prayer and the Sword of the Spirit as spiritual weapons used to overcome relationship strongholds.

Do not believe the hype, there is power in prayer!! It is imperative to put that disclaimer or truth statement out there. Society would have us thinking prayer is not effective to combating the social ills and atrocities of this world. The devil is a liar! Prayer is the first answer. Prayer changes things. Prayer is communion with God and acknowledgement that you need His guidance, wisdom, strength, power, and presence in your life. We must turn to God. As believers, the Word of God instructs us to pray without ceasing. Some may ask why do you pray? My response would be, "the prayers of the righteous avails."

> Scripture: "Is anyone among you in trouble? Let them pray. Is anyone happy? Let them sing songs of praise. Is anyone among you sick? Let them call the elders of the church to pray over them and anoint them with oil in the name of the Lord. And the prayer offered in faith will make the sick person well; the Lord will raise them up. If they have sinned, they will be forgiven. Therefore confess your sins to each other and pray for each other so that you may be healed. The prayer of a righteous person is powerful and effective." -James 5:13-16 NIV

It is important to develop a prayer regime. Being a morning person, I can accomplish more, the earlier I start. Most of this book was written at 3am or 4am just to provide some perspective. Nonetheless, ask God to guide you in developing your routine. Prayer does not always have to be structured. I believe there should be moments in which you spontaneously worship and pray to God. However, it is wise to set aside time to spend in the presence of the Lord as you can get easily get distracted with what the day brings. Intentionality serves one best.

God revealed to me that when I pray, I should declare His word. His word is His will. God hearkens to His word and it will not return to Him empty. God's word is the Sword of the Spirit. If you think of a sword in the natural sense, it is an offensive weapon to protect you from what is coming your way. Generally, the sharper the blade, the stronger the cutting power. This is the same in the spiritual sense. Hebrews 4:12 reads "for the word of God is quick, and powerful, and sharper than any two-edged sword. Piercing even to the dividing asunder of soul and spirit and of the joints and marrow, and is a discerner of the thoughts and intents of the heart." Guard your heart with the Word of God. Read and meditate on it. Meditation is not just sitting in silence. It involves focusing on God's word and applying it to every area of your life. The word of God corrects, empowers, teaches, and helps us align with God's will. Moreover, the word of God is healing. Psalms 107:19-20 reads, "Then they cry unto the Lord in their trouble, and he saveth them out of their distresses. He sent his word, and healed them, and delivered them from their destructions." The Holy Spirit will make the word of God come alive in us so we can apply it to life's challenges and obtain healing and deliverance.

Scripture: "Keep this Book of the Law always on your lips; meditate on it day and night, so that you may be careful to do everything written in it. Then you will be prosperous and successful." –Joshua 1:8 NIV

Scripture: "So is my word that goes out from my mouth: It will not return to me empty, but will accomplish what I desire and achieve the purpose for which I sent it."- Isaiah 55:11 NIV

In addition to the weapons mentioned above, God has given us spiritual strategies to fight against the wiles of the enemy and destroy strongholds: the blood of Jesus and His holy name. Everything must come subject to the name of Jesus.

"And they overcame him by the blood of the Lamb, and by the word of their testimony; and they loved not their lives unto the death." -Revelation 12:11 KJV

"And these signs will accompany those who believe: In my name they will drive out demons; they will speak in new tongues; they will pick up snakes with their hands; and when they drink deadly poison, it will not hurt them at all; they will place their hands on sick people, and they will get well."
-Mark 16:17-18 NIV

"The name of the Lord is a strong tower; the righteous man runs into it and is safe."
-Proverbs 18:10 ESV

Thus far, we have learned anything we value above God can become a stronghold in our minds. Acknowledging and understanding the relationship was a stronghold in your life is not speaking negatively of your partner but speaking more about your mindset and level of spiritual maturity at the time. Notice I stated, "was a stronghold". This was deliberate because as I write this book, I am declaring, in the name of Jesus, that everyone reading this book is free from relationship strongholds. I decree, you will no longer be bound by negative distortions that perpetuate lies and keep you captive. From this day forward, you will begin to challenge every negative thought to the obedience of Christ. You will continue to grow spiritually and walk in your identity in Christ. Amen.

As we discuss relationship strongholds, there must be acknowledgment of sexual immortality. I had to understand engaging in those acts were not in line with the Word of God. We must daily surrender our will to His will and way. God called us to be holy according to His standard. Sexual purity is the standard. This was a challenge for me to grasp. I know God designed sex for marriage; however, after experiencing something intended to be pleasurable, it was difficult to take a vow of purity. But we serve a Mighty God who can deliver. This step also requires much intentionality, and it starts with utilizing the weapons God has given us. When sexual desires entered my mind, I would plead the blood of Jesus then refocus my attention. Sounds simple, right? It was not, especially in the beginning. My first few attempts were unsuccessful, and I found myself going down a path of sin; however, the more you continue to acknowledge God even in your faults, He will strengthen you and uphold you with his righteous hand. It gets easier! I was so proud of myself the first time. I resisted the temptation and overcame the desire. I could not help but praise God, knowing each day I acknowledge Him, I become more like Jesus.

"Scripture: "It is God's will that you should be sanctified: that you should avoid sexual immorality; that each of you should learn to control your own body in a way that is holy and honorable, not in passionate lust like the pagans, who do not know God;" -1 Thessalonians 4:3-5 NIV

Scripture: "For God has not called us to impurity, but to holiness [to be dedicated, and set apart by behavior that pleases Him, whether in public or in private]." -1 Thessalonians 4:7 AMP

Scripture: "So then they that are in the flesh cannot please God" -Romans 8:8 KJV

Scripture: "Submit yourselves therefore to God. Resist the devil, and he will flee from you. Draw nigh to God, and he will draw nigh to you. Cleanse your hands, ye sinners; and purify your hearts, ye double minded." -James 4:7-8 KJV

Scripture: "Seek ye the Lord while he may be found, call ye upon him while he is near: Let the wicked forsake his way, and

the unrighteous man his thoughts: and let him return unto the
Lord, and he will have mercy upon him; and to our God, for he
will abundantly pardon." -Isaiah 55:6-7 KJV

The more you practice using God's weapons to challenge situations in life; you become more sensitive to His voice. Do not get discouraged, keep seeking God. Your deliverance is in drawing near to Him. With this new level of insight, you can cry out to Lord with a humble and repentant heart. He is faithful to perform and be what you need him to be.

What I desire is that God enlightens the eyes of your understanding to recognize you do not have to remain in your current mental state. You are an overcomer because Christ overcame the world, and He lives inside of you. God is all powerful in the heavens and the earth. He is more than able to deliver you! He promised, "When you pass through the waters, I will be with you; and when you pass through the rivers, they will not sweep over you. When you walk through the fire, you will not be burned; the flames will not set you ablaze." (Isaiah 43:2, NIV). When seeking God, He will show you which strategy to use for the most optimal outcome.

Poem - Takeover

Let divine revelation of who you are within me unveil itself
Takeover Jesus
That I might think how you think
Takeover my mind
That I might express love like you Jesus
Take over my spirit
That I might live how you lived Jesus according to God's will
Takeover my body
Takeover, takeover, takeover
That I may KNOW you and be Christ like in every aspect of my life.
Takeover my eyes, ears, mouth, limbs, desires, dreams, purpose
Let every aspect of my being align with your will for my life.
Takeover Jesus

TOTAL SURRENDER TO GOD

For God to takeover, you must fully surrender to him. This requires a daily sacrifice of your flesh. Jesus said in Luke 9:23 reads "if any man will come after me, let him deny himself, and take up his cross daily and follow me." This is a daily process of submission to God's will over your life. Begin to reflect on what has hindered you from submitting your all to the Lord. When asked that question my mouth was filled with reasons…. "My rejection, my fear, my self-doubt, my limitations, my lack of willingness to take accountability," all flowed out. At the end of the day, it was all excuses. I am stopping myself!

Exercise

Self-reflection and self-evaluation are crucial tools one must undertake in their walk with Christ. Corinthians 13:5 reads "examine yourselves, whether ye be in the faith; prove your own selves".

Ask yourself, what is stopping me from completely surrendering to God?

_____

_____

_____

_____

_____

_____

_____

_____

_____

_____

_____

Poem – So You Think

So you think you got this all figured out, huh
You got these big plans
Where you're going
Who you're going to be with
Have you taken the time to acknowledge me?
I mean I only created the universe in 7 days
The sun, the moon, and the stars
I only commanded the world with one phrase "Let there be"
I only know how many follicles of hair lay on your head
I only know how your heartbeat
I only know your thoughts before you form them
I only created you for a divine purpose and that's the reason you are still walking on this earth
I only sent my son in the form of a man to die on the cross so you might be reconciled back to me and have eternal life
I only love you unconditionally although your love for me has conditions
I only wipe the tears from your eyes and hold you in the midnight hour when life appears to be caving in
I only listen to you murmur and complain and still bless you.
But God I'm broke with a broke down car and low paying job and a roof caving in.
You still alive aren't you??? You are blessed!
I am only the one who takes your insecurities and whisper in your ear "you are my chosen one, you are my seed, you are my creation and I made you perfect"

So you think you can do this without acknowledging me? Your Abba father
The beginning and the end
Omnipresent and omniscient
The ruler of the world
The ultimate judge.
So you think?

Proverbs 19:21 reads, "many are the plan's in a person's heart, but it is the Lord's purpose that prevails. Lord, let your purpose for my life reign supreme; prove more powerful than any other desire in my heart.

The above poem came to me in the years prior to writing this book. As I started to follow God's plan, I began to understand what He was revealing to me. God was speaking directly to me about by life choices. I have always prided myself in the ability to make a goal, set a plan, and achieve the desired result. The difference was I was reliant on my own strength not understanding it was God who placed those desires inside of me. He gave me the strength and determination to accomplish the task. Dependence on my own strength, only took me so far. As we begin to develop spiritually and daily surrender to God's will, we must totally depend on Him to guide us. We have plans in life and that is totally fine; however, those plans should not take precedence over our purpose in life. We were created to serve God and carry out His purpose. Thus, our plans, visions, thoughts, and actions should be in total alignment with our purpose. God is Jehovah Rohi - He is our Shepherd who leads and guides us to the path of righteousness. Thus, we can trust and believe if we allow our purpose to prevail, we will achieve those innermost desires. The Word states, God will give us the desires of our heart if we delight in Him. We must take pleasure in knowing God's rewards are eternal and extend from everlasting to everlasting.

Scripture: But seek ye first the kingdom of God, and his righteousness; and all these things shall be added unto you.
–Matthew 6:33 KJV

Delight thyself also in the Lord; and he shall give thee the desires of thine heart. Commit thy way unto the Lord; trust also in him; and he shall bring it to pass. -Psalms 37:4-5 KJV

"The best it yet to come in your decision-making"
-Prophetic word from Pastor Shay

The more time I spent with God, the more I noticed a change in my desires. Things that were once thrilling, no longer excited me. I no longer needed the temporal feeling that came with partying, alcohol, and sex. After I indulged in those things, I still felt empty and alone. I felt as if something was missing in my life. I felt meaningless. Which is why the Word of God instructs us to hunger and thirst after righteous for true fulfillment. The decision to follow God was the best decision I have ever made. For, He is the best thing that ever happened to me. God began to place new desires in my heart that He set out to fulfill. As my desires began to shift, I also became stronger in my conviction this was not the relationship God designed for me. As I surrendered more to God; He gave me the strength to break away. There were times, in which I wanted to go back to what was familiar to me. The fear of the unknown had me bound. However, God confirmed His word in a prophetic voice. "The best it yet to come in your decision-making".

As we surrender to God, we must examine the choices we make. The decisions you make impact generations to come. One man's decision to be faithful to God resulted in a multi-generational legacy and promise God fulfilled. Abraham obeyed God and received an inheritance which applied to his descendants that were as many as the dust of the earth. Do you know you are a part of that inheritance? God began to reveal more to Abraham when he obeyed and trusted Him. God rewards obedience. Moses was devoted to God, His cause, and preemptive will. This devotion led to Moses seeing the Glory of God. God considered Moses His friend and changed His course of action towards the children of Israel at the request of Moses (Read Exodus 32 and 33). In contrast, your decisions could lead to death and destruction. In Joshua the 7th chapter, we learn, Anchan's failure to follow God's instructions in the journey to the promise land led to his death and his children. The consequences of our choices impact our children and future generations. Make daily decisions that honor and glorify God! Allow God to have total preeminence in your daily decision making. Ask yourself, is this conducive towards my walk with Christ? Will this decision honor God? Consider the legacy you want to leave. Does this decision represent your legacy? Choose wisely.

Scripture: Trust in the Lord with all thine heart; and lean not unto thine own understanding. In all thy ways acknowledge him, and he shall direct thy paths. Be not wise in your own eyes, fear the Lord, and turn away from evil. It will be healing to your flesh and refreshment to your bones.
–Proverbs 3:5-6 KJV

Devotion to God is always the best and most worthwhile decision you could ever make. What a privilege and an honor it is to worship at the throne of God: To partake in the advancement of His purpose and will. It is not like He needs our help, but he grants us access into His kingdom for our benefits. Some of the benefits of devotion to God include a sense of being, purpose, favor, grace, peace, true happiness, healing, and comfort. Everything we need, He is. It is only right that you are devoted to someone who can freely give you everything you need. That void you are feeling inside will only be fulfilled by God. Jesus said in John 4:14 "But whosoever drinketh of the water that I shall give him shall never thirst; but the water that I shall give him shall be in him a well of water springing up into everlasting life." Your spirit will be fed when you pursue your first love.

Poem- The Pursuit

You are everything I want and need
The attentiveness you provide
You have a special way of making me feel like I am all that matters
A unique way of making me feel loved
You exceed my expectations
The satisfaction, joy, and peace I receive in your presence
extends far above any earthly interaction
Your presence brightens my darkest days
Every encounter with you is a privilege
Appeasing to my soul.
Even in moments of chastisement, You're still gentle.
I don't have to mask my feelings
I feel like I can take on the world
I have strength like a lion
I can soar high like an eagle
I feel wise as an ant
So as a deer pants for the water, I pursue you Father
My soul chases after you with longing to sense you, to hear you,
To see you, to be more like you
You are my pursuit

Chapter Three

⤳ Devotion — Choosing Yourself ⤳

"In this moment I choose to draw my attention to the present moment. I chose not to focus on the past or over anticipate the future."
I choose me…

This chapter focuses on making a conscious effort towards self-betterment; Allowing God to guide and build you up on your most holy faith. It will include tools and various contemplative practices that were instrumental in my healing process. This chapter details what was effective in my journey. I cannot reiterate enough the importance of seeking God for direction in your healing process.

Self-care is important when healing from relationships. Self-care simply means "I choose me." God cares about our total well-being (emotional, physical, and mental). He is concerned with every detail of our lives. 1 Thessalonians 5:23 reads, "And the very God of peace sanctify you wholly; and I pray God your whole spirit and soul and body be preserved blameless unto the coming of our Lord Jesus Christ." Thus, it is not God's will for us to be strong and disciplined in one area and struggling in others. God finds pleasure in the prosperity of His people (Psalms 35:27). He desires for us to succeed and prosper in every area.

∼ Exercise ∼

Begin to think about what makes you smile? What soothes you? Ask God to guide you on how you can incorporate those activities into your schedule on a daily, weekly, monthly, and yearly basis. For me, taking bubble baths and reading a good book is very relaxing. I also enjoy nature walks and just breathing in God's creation. These are practical activities I can do on a more consistent basis whereas taking a vacation may be an annual goal. Begin to develop a checklist of things that bring you pleasure. Formulate a plan to start doing those things on an ongoing basis.

_____

_____

_____

_____

_____

_____

_____

_____

_____

_____

Self-care also encompasses attending to your wounds. The first hurt that comes to mind is childhood trauma. Trauma is defined as a psychological, or emotional response to an experience that is deeply distressing or disturbing (Center for Anxiety and Mood Disorders, 2018). Long term exposure to childhood trauma has the capacity to impact brain functioning. This is typically contingent upon the intensity, duration, and frequency of the traumatic experience. Childhood trauma is critical because the brain is rapidly developing during those early years potentially increasing the likelihood of lifelong effects. Nonetheless, an important takeaway is how our past experiences tend to dictate how we respond to stress later in life. This explains why two people experiencing the exact same traumatic situation, could respond totally opposite of one another. Some can become more resilient in those circumstances and others may experience emotional and behavioral dysregulation.

Since everyone has unique life experiences, their mechanisms for coping with a breakup are different. However, God's word is true, and we can all actively attack our old wounds with His instruction. We must ask God to examine the most inner parts of our hearts and reveal what is the underlying root cause of the challenges we face. God showed me that I was dealing with the spirit of rejection and how it impacted several decisions I had made throughout the course of my life. I was allowing my fear of rejection to guide my decision-making. In the spirit of transparency, God is dealing with me as I write this book on not being consumed by what others will think or what I believe others would want to hear, but to totally depend on Him. I was not to rely on my knowledge, degrees, or professional certifications, but look to Jesus the author and finisher of my faith. In ministry, we often think will others receive what I have to offer. I had a habit of second guessing myself. The Holy Spirit dealt with my insecurities and revealed to me second guessing myself was second guessing Him. It is through Him that we move, live, and have our being. If I am allowing God to use me as a living vessel, why am I questioning my capabilities? This is how the Holy Spirit gracefully corrects us.

Poem - Letter to Rejection.

Rejection,

Why have thou kept me burdened so long
From my days as a young child.
These memories have flooded my mind oh so gently but aggressively.

A constant perception will I ever me good enough.
Relationships, purpose, spirituality, parenting.
Am I enough?
How do I surpass my insecurities?
God says, before I knew thee, I formed thee and made you perfect.
You are loved
You are wanted
You have my stamp of approval
I called thee by name to be a blessing to many
You are not rejected, for you are justified by my Son's blood
The Blood of Jesus that makes us all worthy
To be welcomed and accepted into the Kingdom of God

Signed, My Identity in Christ Jesus

Most of my poetry are conversations with God. They begin with how I am feeling or thinking in the moment but ends with what the Word of God says about the situation. This is the application of taking on the amour of God (Sword of the Spirit) to actively attack our situations and challenges in life. God's word will not return to Him void but will accomplish the task He desires. As previously stated, God takes pleasure in our prosperity. He does not desire for us to be bound by any demonic spirit, which is why we can sit with our emotions (acknowledge how we are feeling) and become vulnerable with God. Allow Him to take care of our emotions.

Acknowledging I struggled with the Spirit of Rejection, was a turnaround point for me. Now, I understood the root cause of my pattern of dysfunction in relationships. I became aware I have attracted men who were struggling with the same spirit. "For we wrestle not against flesh and blood, but against principalities, against powers, against the rulers of the darkness of this world, against spiritual wickedness in high places" (Ephesians 6:12). We learned earlier that this is a spiritual battle. Thus, we cannot fight with carnal weapons, but we must utilize the amour of God to withstand. Do not allow your life experiences dictate how you respond to stressors in life. Allow the Word of God to guide your responses. The dark areas in your life are spiritual battles that require divine intervention to overcome. We all have issues or internal battles that we daily suppress. Albeit the pain we feel, chose to breathe, and take it all in. Acknowledge, expose, and release it. God will heal it. Thus, walk in victory and declare, "I am set free from every demonic hindrance and attack. I am guaranteed victory through Christ Jesus." Prior to coming into the realization that I struggled with rejection, my former partner acknowledged he did not respond well to rejection. In knowing we both struggled with the spirit of rejection, I recognized we were never good for each other, because we were not good enough for ourselves. Therefore, I would continue to repeat the pattern of dysfunction until I was delivered from the spirit that had be bound.

∼≋ Exercise ≋∼

Pray and ask God to search your heart. Ask Him to reveal to you the most inward parts. Record your revelations.

Scripture: Search me, O God, and know my heart; try me, and know my thoughts: And see there be any wicked way in me, and lead me in the way everlasting -Psalms 139: 23-24 KJV

Scripture: Behold, You desire truth in the most innermost being, and in the hidden part of my heart. You will make me know wisdom. Purify me with hyssop, and I will be clean; wash me, and I will be whiter than snow. –Psalms 51:6-7 AMP

_____

_____

_____

_____

_____

_____

_____

_____

_____

Poem - K.I.S.S. Me

Look deeply in my eyes
Handle me with care
Approach me with grace
A stare so intense that pierce my soul
Express to me Your desires
Teach me your likes and dislikes
K.I.S.S. me
Grab my hand
Console me after a challenging day
Let me know everything will be ok
Nurture me with Your love
K.I.S.S. me
A touch so endearing
Electrifying, with great fulfillment
A kiss of death of my old ways
A kiss of fate to eternal life
K.I.S.S. me
Kind Intense Soul Searching

SELF-CARE: UTILIZING CONTEMPLATIVE PRACTICES

Sometimes, people need additional tools to begin the process of healing. A new concept in clinical practice is mindfulness. Mindfulness is the ability to focus your attention on the present moment. Mindfulness is defined as purposely and nonjudgmentally paying attention to the present moment (Kabat-Zinn, 2003). This can be further described as the direct awareness of what you are doing, feeling, or thinking as it occurs in the moment. Therefore, you can practice mindfulness at any time. The application of mindfulness begins with the breath as an anchor for our attention. At times, during the practice, our attention will wander, but we notice it along with our reactions, and then nonjudgmentally return our attention back to the sensation of the breath. As you continue to exercise mindfulness meditation, you will notice the cycle becomes easier and your mind wanders less frequently. The ongoing practice of mindfulness expands attention association areas of the brain and as a result leads to decreases in activity in the prefrontal cortex responsible for emotional responses, decisions, planning, and judging[1]. In addition, focusing on the breath activates structures in the nervous systems such as the hypothalamus, hippocampus, and amygdala, flooding the body with chemicals responsible for self-regulation and positive feeling[1]. In this state of awareness, you can have a clearer and more alert mind. Essentially, mindfulness is mental training.

Mindfulness originated from eastern philosophies but has become more popular with mainstream media and endorsements from celebrities. Some may shy away from various contemplative practices based on its origins, and feelings of shame and guilt. One may think acknowledging you are stress and choosing mindfulness as a form of stress management can imply you are not relying on God's ability to rescue you. As a Believer, I was able to utilize the practice to heighten my spiritual awareness and realize the importance of choosing myself because I am worth it. We all are worth it!

The more I studied mindfulness, God revealed to me how meditation practices were congruent to biblical text or terminology such as:

- Genesis 2:7 which emphasizes deep breathing
- Genesis 13:12-14 - Imagery and Visualization
- Psalms 26:2-3 - Reflective journaling after a period of attunement and silence.
- Psalms 46:10 - Stillness and letting go
- Joshua 1:8 - Meditation

These are just the obvious texts. There are so many scriptures throughout God's word that typifies mindfulness. As a result, I was able to embrace mindfulness because God has given all humans the capacity to grasp concepts that are true, even if the underlying philosophies are different. As Believers, we can embrace the practice of mindfulness by drawing from our own faith traditions.

One exercise that has been primarily helpful an increasing awareness of God's presence and self, is mindful breathing. When faced with stressful situations, take a moment to pause/**_Stop_**. **_Take_** three deep breaths. **_Observe_** your reactions. Is your heart racing? Do you feel uneasiness in the stomach? Are your palms sweaty? After you become aware of what is going on in your body and around you, **_proceed_**.

Taking the moment to S.T.O.P. (s=stop, t=take a breath, o=observe, p=proceed) before you act, helps us to respond positively to situation versus reacting negatively.

MY SAFE PLACE

I often spoke with my clients about the power of entering a safe place in moments of distress. If you feel your warning signs are shooting red lights, stop, take a deep breath, and enter your safe place. Entering your safe place shifts your focus and energy towards something that brings you joy and delight, and literally brings you to a place that feels protected. When I finally had proof of the infidelity in my relationship, I was an emotional wreck. I questioned by abilities. How could God bless me with the gift of teaching, an advocate for mental healing and peace, when my mind was in turmoil? How can I train people on inner peace when I do not have any myself? In that instance, I chose to acknowledge my emotions instead of hindering it. I began to write all my feelings in a journal and describe why I felt that way. Well, that was a boost; however, my spirit was still troubled because I could not let go of the why? Why me? Why now? In that moment, I had to make a choice: Do I allow my emotions to overtake me? No! Instead, I chose to sit with my emotions and walk towards complete healing. God led me to pray; however, I needed to separate from the environment that was bringing me pain to fully feel safe. God further directed me to take a walk.

HAVE A LITTLE TALK WITH JESUS...

During my walk, I had a little talk with Jesus... I began with praise. Despite my circumstances, I was still alive, and He was still God. I began to rehearse my victories. When I felt I was at my lowest point after the death of my grandfather, God delivered me. He heard my cry. I asked Him to wrap his loving arms around me and he came in person and held me. When I was going to lose my home, he spoke to me in a gentle voice and said, "it would be alright". He had delivered me out of those circumstances, so I was confident He was able. He is the same God! I profusely cried tears of joy. The enemy tried to take my mind, but I chose not to allow it. As a result, God allowed his presence to overtake me. By praising Him, I was reactivating my faith. Who would imagine after learning about infidelity, I was at peace? How amazing is our God!

I discovered my safe place is in the presence of God. For, "the name of the Lord is a strong tower: the righteous run to it and is safe and set on high (far above evil)" (Proverbs 18:10, AMP). The scripture reads those who run to it are safe, which means you must move quickly towards God. The ability to say I am going to call on the name of the Lord, and not allow individuals or situations to change my emotions, is easier said than done. It takes daily practice. Nonetheless, God provides perfect instructions of how to deal with your emotions and enter his presence when you are in distress.

Scripture:
1 I cried out to God for help: I cried out to God to hear me.
2 When I was in distress, I sought the Lord; at night I stretched out untiring hands, and I would not be comforted.
3 I remembered you, God, and I groaned; I meditated, and my spirit grew faint.
4 You kept my eyes from closing; I was too troubled to speak.
5 I thought about the former days, the years of long ago.
6 I remembered my songs in the night. My heart meditated and my spirit asked:
7 "Will the Lord reject forever? Will he never show his favor again?
8 Has his unfailing love vanished forever?   Has his promise failed for all time?
9 Has God forgotten to be merciful?   Has he in anger withheld his compassion?"
10 Then I thought, "To this I will appeal: the years when the Most High stretched out his right hand.
11 I will remember the deeds of the Lord; yes, I will remember your miracles of long ago.
12 I will consider all your works and meditate on all your mighty deeds."
13 Your ways, God, are holy. What god is as great as our God?
14 You are the God who performs miracles; you display your power among the peoples.
15 With your mighty arm you redeemed your people, the descendants of Jacob and Joseph.
16 The waters saw you, God, the waters saw you and writhed; he very depths were convulsed.
17 The clouds poured down water, the heavens resounded with thunder; your arrows flashed back and forth.
18 Your thunder was heard in the whirlwind, lightning lit up the

world; the earth trembled and quaked.
19 Your path led through the sea, your way through the mighty
waters, though your footprints were not seen.
20 You led your people like a flock by the hand of Moses and
Aaron. *Psalms 77: 1-20, KJV*

In the scripture, the psalmist was in complete distress and could not find evidence that God was responding to him. He felt as if God had forsaken him. Right in the middle of the passage you see a shift in the psalmist's attitude in which God begins to activate his faith. He challenged his negative distortions by rehearsing his victories. You may find yourself in similar situations, especially as you experience feelings of grief and loss in a relationship. However, I challenge you to take on the same attitude and continue to commune with God. Draw your attention to His goodness, past acts of love, and victories. Praise him in your distress. We are assured he will hear and deliver us.

Scripture: This poor man cried, and the Lord heard him, and saved him out of all his troubles. Psalms 34:6, KJV
Scripture: "The righteous cry out, and the Lord hears them; he delivers them from all their troubles. The Lord is close to the brokenhearted and saves those who are crushed in spirit. The righteous person may have many troubles, but the Lord delivers him from them all;"- Psalms 34:17-19 NIV

Poem – "I Have Someplace to Go"

I have some place to go.
When I feel lonely in despair, I have some place to go.
When my emotions are spiraling out of control, I have some place to go
when my stomach is experiencing uneasiness due to worrying and stress, I have some place to go.
When I seek the attention of people and experience disappointment.
When I allow desperation to compromise my wholeness.
When I don't feel whole but with a broken spirit and a contrite heart, I have some place to go

Thank you, Jesus, for giving me the mind to enter your presence. A place where I can be vulnerable with my Heavenly

Father and immediately feel the weight lifted off my shoulder. I chose to draw nigh unto you Father Your presence is my place to go. And instantaneously, God begins to open the eyes of my understanding and expand my perspective. I realize I have so much to be thankful for. With a heart of thanksgiving, I begin to bless your name. I focus my attention on your goodness and your miraculous work. Your doings are marvelous in my eyes. Your name is worthy of all the praise, honor, and glory. At the name of Jesus, every knee shall bow every tongue shall confess you are God. So, I surrender my speech/confession to you Father and declare I will honor and praise Your name right now. I don't want no rock crying out for me. You are totally worthy of my worship. I am privileged to enter your presence for you turned a moment of sadness into joy and gladness. In your presence there is fullness of joy and at your right-hand pleasures forevermore. Thank you, Father, for the realization that I have some place to go.

We know our safe place is truly in the presence of God. In the presence of God, we can find fullness of joy. I encourage you to seek God for an area in which you feel peace. Designate that area as a place where you can experience the uninterrupted presence of God.

All the tools that I discussed in this chapter, were divinely inspired for an appointed time. God led me to study mindfulness, discover my safe place, and learn how to respond to stress, because He knew my struggles. He knew the best way for me to overcome them. This is why it is important to devote your energy towards God first. He knows you best. He is your Creator.

PART II

DEVOTION

CHAPTER FOUR

⌒DEVOTION — TRUSTING THE PROCESS⌒

"My problems are small and irrelevant because God, the Creator of the universe, is with me!"

This is the step that requires the most discipline and commitment. There are five key stages to trusting the process: 1.) Acknowledgment 2.) Identification of your Thought Process 3.) Acceptance 4.) Waiting/Divine Development 5.) Wholeness/Spiritual Restoration

1.) ACKNOWLEDGEMENT

During this stage you will go through a range of emotions: anger, bitterness, regret, despair, strive. Sometimes you cannot describe how you feel. There is nothing there like numbness. Pray that God begins to soften your heart to receive him and grant you wisdom to understand what is truly going on in your body. Your emotions, thoughts, and feelings are all connected. When you can verbalize what you are experiencing, you are walking towards your healing. God cannot heal what you do not acknowledge.

Become vulnerable with God and acknowledge how you feel. Hebrews 4:16 instruct us to come boldly before the throne of grace, that we may obtain grace and mercy in the time of need. Tell God about your pain and hurt. Trust that he hears your cry and will deliver you. In my moments of distress, I realized I could not be truly honest with anyone, but God. That openness was the gateway to my healing. It was like a small voice saying, "be upfront with yourself and speak from your inner being." Release your emotions. Allow God to take care of your emotions for He cares for you. My mother always says God is concerned about EVERYTHING that concerns you. What I love about God, is that He will give you a sign that he hears your cry and plea. This is confidence that we have, God responds to our cries.

> Scriptures: "The Lord is close to the brokenhearted and saves those who are crushed in spirit."-Psalms 34:18 NIV
>
> "For he will deliver the needy who cry out, the afflicted who have no one to help."-Psalms 72:12 NIV
>
> "The righteous cry out, and the Lord hears them; he delivers them from all their troubles."-Psalms 34:17 NIV

In addition, God led me to journal my experiences to deal with my hurt. By journaling, I was able to acknowledge my emotions and in those moments of vulnerability God would reveal Himself to me. I encourage you all to have a journal and begin to document your journey. Highlight your feelings, your prayers, the lessons learned, and your victories. Ask God to lead you for sometimes we do not know what to say, write, or even pray. Nevertheless, when you acknowledge God, He will begin to speak through you. The core of this book is a compilation of my journaling, conversations with God, and revelations received from studying the Word. He turned my writings which I thought at the time was intended to help me overcome my relationship into a book that would help others. God is amazing!

2.) IDENTIFICATION OF YOUR THOUGHT PROCESS

In Cognitive Behavioral Therapy, therapist delve deeper into a person's thoughts and how it manifests into certain behaviors. As the Bible states. "So, a man thinketh, that he is". My thoughts after the breakup ranged from "why me?" to "what's wrong with me? Instead of rehearsing those negative distortions, God led me to declare:

> "I'm fearfully and wonderfully made my God. Handcrafted, His perfection creation. I am one of a kind. I have God's DNA. I am choosing to rely on God's infinite and faultless wisdom and trust his plans. My wisdom is limited, and I do not know everything; however, God knows and sees all. He could be saving/protecting me from a lifetime of heartache."

∼ Exercise ∼

You may experience moments in which you feel inadequate and insecure because the relationship is ending and find yourself asking similar questions. Was I good enough? Will I ever find someone to love me? Am I worthy of love?

Begin to record those negative thoughts. Some writing points to consider: What are your thoughts about the relationship? What triggers those distortions? How has your thoughts manifested into action?

_____

_____

_____

_____

_____

_____

_____

_____

_____

_____

Now that you have identified your thought process, begin to challenge it with the word of God and the leading of the Holy Spirit. The first step in challenging negative thinking is knowing what God says about you. The scriptures you recorded earlier provided a great starting point. Begin to meditate on scriptures about God's love. Below are some additional scriptures that you can focus on:

The Lord hath appeared of old unto me, saying, Yea, I have loved thee with an everlasting love: therefore with loving kindness have I drawn thee. - Jeremiah 31:3, KJV
Give thanks to the God of heaven. His love endures forever. -Psalms 136:26, NIV

For the mountains may depart and the hills be removed, but my steadfast love shall not depart from you, and my covenant of peace shall not be removed," says the LORD, who has compassion on you. -Isaiah 54:10, ESV

Because your steadfast love is better than life, my lips will praise you.- Psalm 63:3, ESV

The Lord, the Lord, a God merciful and gracious, slow to anger, and abounding in steadfast love and faithfulness, keeping steadfast love for thousands, forgiving iniquity and transgression and sin. - Exodus 34:6-7, ESV

In overflowing anger for a moment I hid my face from you, but with everlasting love I will have compassion on you," says the LORD, your Redeemer. -Isaiah 54:8, ESV

Nor height nor depth, nor anything else in all creation, will be able to separate us from the love of God in Christ Jesus our Lord. - Romans 8:39, ESV

Not only does God love us unconditionally, but He demonstrated his love by giving us the greatest gift of all- salvation through His son Jesus Christ!

For God so loved the world, that he gave his only Son, that whoever believes in him should not perish but have eternal life.

-John 3:16, ESV

But God shows his love for us in that while we were still sinners, Christ died for us. -Romans 5:8, ESV

In this was manifested the love of God toward us, because that God sent his only begotten Son into the world, that we might live through him. -1 John 4:9, KJV

God will never stop loving you! Although the relationship was deemed a failure by man's standard you can rest assured God's love never fails. In those times when you begin to question your capacities and capabilities, focus on God's word. Philippians 4:16 instructs, "Finally, brethren, whatsoever things are true, whatsoever things are honest, whatsoever things are just, whatsoever things are pure, whatsoever things are lovely, whatsoever things are of good report; if there be any virtue, and if there be any praise, think on these things. God's love is true. His love is pure, honest, and just. His love encompasses all the characteristics listed above and more. Focus on His Love.

LEARNING THE LESSON

Exercise

God makes no mistakes. Everything you experience in life can be taken as a lesson. Ask God to shift your mindset about the relationship, not to view it as a failure or something wrong, but a lesson learned. Ask yourself, what did I learn? What did this relationship teach me about myself? How do I want to be treated? What expectations will I set in the next relationship as a result of the lessons learned? Record your responses below.

_____

_____

_____

_____

_____

_____

_____

_____

_____

Afterwards, make another declaration: "I will no longer cry over what I have perceived as a loss, but instead focus my attention on what I have gained. Nothing is lost in the Kingdom, for God is my Restorer and will grant me beauty for my ashes and oil for my joy."

Poem - "I Can Reach You"

Hanging on to life by a thread
I'm unsure of where to go
I stretched my hands so I can reach you
If I can just touch you Jesus, I know I will make it.
I know I will be made whole
I can achieve heights unknown
If I can just reach you
Draw nigh to me Jesus
I need to feel you
Allow me to feel your closeness.
Let me know you love me.
Let me know you care
Endow me with your presence, grab my hand
Jesus, pull me into your presence safe from all harm.
So the rough edges of life become smooth.
The unbearable become peaceful
Where I no longer cry for what I have lost
Instead I receive beauty for ashes.
Oil for my joy.
Where my deliverance and restoration lie.
Comfort me with understanding that this experience will not overtake me.
Caress me with you nail scarred hands to remind me my victory is predestined.
Reassure me You're not far away
for you live inside of me
Let me know I can reach you.

Scripture: The Spirit of the Lord God is upon me; because the Lord hath anointed me to preach good tidings unto the meek; he hath sent me to bind up the brokenhearted, to proclaim liberty to the captives, and the opening of the prison to them that are bound;
2To proclaim the acceptable year of the Lord, and the day of vengeance of our God; to comfort all that mourn;

3 To appoint unto them that mourn in Zion, to give unto them beauty for ashes, the oil of joy for mourning, the garment of praise for the spirit of heaviness; that they might be called trees of righteousness, the planting of the Lord, that he might be glorified. - Isaiah 61:1-3, KJV

PREDESTINED BY GOD

It is also important to understand everything you go through in life is for a purpose. Just as God has predestined our victories, He also predestined our experiences, all for His glory. God knew what we would go through. For we do not have a High Priest who is unable to empathize with our weaknesses, but we have one who has been tempted in every way, just as we are--yet He did not sin (Hebrew 4:15). He knows our heartaches, disappointments, insecurities, hurt, and pain. Yet, His power is greater than anything we could ever experience, and He has guaranteed our victory through Jesus Christ. We can stand firm knowing, through our experiences God is molding us to become the best version of ourselves in Christ. I can confidently declare my next chapter will be my best chapter and take on a spirit of gratitude for this period of divine development.

Scripture: "Before I formed you in the womb I knew you, before you were born I set you apart; I appointed you as a prophet to the nations."-Jeremiah 1:5 NIV

Scripture: Ye have not chosen me, but I have chosen you, and ordained you, that ye should go and bring forth fruit, and that your fruit should remain: that whatsoever ye shall ask of the Father in my name, he may give it you. - John 15:16, KJV

Scripture: In whom also we have obtained an inheritance, being predestinated according to the purpose of him who worketh all things after the counsel of his own will –Ephesians 1:11 KJV

Scripture: And we know that all things work together for good to them that love God, to them who are the called according to his purpose. For whom he did foreknow, he also did predestinate to be conformed to the image of his Son, that he might be the firstborn among many brethren. Moreover whom he did predestinate, them he also called: and whom he called, them he also justified: and whom he justified, them he also glorified. What shall we then say to these things? If God be for us, who can be against us? He that spared not his own Son, but delivered him up for us all, how shall he not with him also freely give us all things?- Romans 8:28-32 KJV

3.) ACCEPTANCE

Psalms 46:10 reads, "Be still, and know that I am God; I will be exalted among the nations, I will be exalted in the earth." The Hebrew meaning of stillness means to let go. Letting go and acceptance are essential attitudes of mindfulness. In the stage above, you will become more aware of your inner experience including intense thoughts and feelings. You may want to hold on to some things and desperately get rid of others. Simply, let it be. Accept what comes up as it is instead of trying to control it. Acceptance indicates you have surrendered control. In trusting the process, you must also recognize the sovereignty of God. God can handle all your hurt, disappointments, insecurities, failures, etc. His eyes run throughout the earth seeking to show himself strong on the behalf of people who are committed to Him. He will be there to take care of you. Accept that you cannot change the outcome. Allow God to change and finish the narrative.

4.) WAITING/DIVINE DEVELOPMENT

Waiting is your period of divine development. In trusting the process, God will help you understand what you go through in life is the period of chastisement. A time in which the Holy Spirit is molding and shaping you into who he has called you to be. Hebrews 12:1 reads, "For the moment all discipline seems painful rather than pleasant, but later it yields the peaceful fruit of righteous to those who trained by it." Hebrews the 12th chapter also instructs us to look to Jesus the author and finisher of our faith as the perfect example of how to trust God in the midst of trials and tribulations. Although it was painful, Jesus endured the cross and now he sits at the right hand of God. While waiting for his purpose to be fulfilled, Jesus prayed, fasted, performed miracles, and spent time with God. In the world's system, waiting has a negative connotation and is viewed as passiveness. Waiting is not passive but actively seeking God until your prayers manifest. Waiting is recognizing God does not need your assistance. Waiting is discipline and focus.

≈ Exercise ≈

Challenge your thoughts about waiting. Below is a practical example of how to reframe your thoughts about your period of divine development.

Thought: Why do I have to wait?
Emotion: Loneliness
Action: Sexual Impurity

Reframe your thoughts: God is developing me into the woman or man of God he has called me to be. I trust his characteristics to be faithful and a rewarder to those who diligently seek Him.

Find scriptures that negate the negative thought.

Example Scriptures:
"The Lord is good to those who wait for him, to the soul who seeks him." -Lamentations 3:25 ESV

"I remain confident of this: I will see the goodness of the Lord in the land of the living. Wait for the Lord; be strong and take heart and wait for the Lord." -Psalms 27:13-14 NIV

_____

_____

_____

_____

_____

_____

Exercise

Poem – "Wait"

Wait I say, wait on the Lord
They that wait on the Lord shall mount up on wings as eagles
Lord, grant me my wings
I want to fly while I wait
I want to soar
I want strength not to fall into the old habits that hindered my growth in You
The desire to be accepted and validated
Habits that compromise my values and lead to actions not pleasing to you Father
Lord, grant me patience to trust the plans You have for my life
For You are my Creator
You know me in and out.
You know what's best for me
Help me to trust Your best for me
While I wait
This period of singleness is the time to learn more of You and myself
The time to focus my attention on what you would have me to do
To seek You all the more
I breathe, I inhale, I exhale
I wait, I practice patience
I trust You, I learn Your will, Your way
Wait I say, for it will happen!

Scripture: Wait on the Lord, and keep his way, and he shall exalt thee to inherit the land: when the wicked are cut off, thou shalt see it. I have seen the wicked in great power, and spreading himself like a green bay tree. Yet he passed away, and, lo, he was not: yea, I sought him, but he could not be found. Mark the perfect man, and behold the upright: for the end of that man is peace. But the transgressors shall be destroyed together: the end of the wicked shall be cut off. But the salvation of the righteous is of the Lord: he is their strength in the time of trouble. And the Lord shall help them, and deliver them: he shall deliver them from the wicked, and save them, because they trust in him." -Psalms 37 KJV

Prayer

God you are omniscient! You are all-knowing. You know our past, present, and future. Help us to trust you with our whole heart and lean not to our own understanding. Help us to acknowledge you in all our decision-making and trust you for an answer. Holy Spirit, we give you permission to remove flesh and sinful desires for it is the gateway to poor decisions. Lord, go before us so that we make daily decisions that honor you. I declare that desperation, fear, and anxiety will no longer guide our choices. God you know the hearts of your people. Some may have the desire for companionship, but we want to wait on you. Help us to crucify flesh while we wait. You are our first and true lover. You know what we want and need. Thus, we trust that you know what and who is best for us. We know it is done in Jesus name. Thank you, Father!

During your period of singleness, there are times in which you experience disappointment and begin to question God's timing. There were moments, in which, I would entertain men to satisfy feelings of loneliness. I knew deep down the relationship was not headed anywhere. I was about to repeat the same pattern. Trust God has his best in store for you! Jesus is the best company! Become satisfied with your decision to devote your energy towards God, and do not allow desperation and fear compromise your wholeness. Trust God's perfect timing throughout this process. 2 Peter 3:8-9 reads, "But do not forget this one thing, dear friends: With the Lord a day is like a thousand years, and a thousand years are like a day. The Lord is not slow in keeping his promise, as some understand slowness. Instead he is patient with you, not wanting anyone to perish, but everyone to come to repentance."

At times, we feel anxious and impatient instead of trusting God's timing. You may have the urge to take matters into your own hands. The word of God says, lean not to your own understanding. We allow our societal values to place God in a box. We put timelines on when things should happen based on what the world believes. God has proven time and time again His timing is not our timing. My grandmother had a phrase speaking of unlimited possibilities we have in God. I can hear her voice so clearly with so much passion and conviction, declaring "TTLOG", **T**aking **T**he **L**imits **O**ff **G**od! He can do the impossible, so this matter is nothing for My God to handle.

Hebrews 10:35-26 reads "So do not throw away your confidence; it will be richly rewarded. You need to persevere so that when you have done the will of God, you will receive what he has promised." Therefore, utilize this time to develop patience and the habit of not comparing yourselves to others. God is not slow to respond to His people. He is an on-time God. Keep on believing as God responds to our faith. Prevail and persist with patience beyond your circumstances and watch God move.

Certainly, there will be nights where you feel lonely in your idle time. However, utilize those moments for your self-care activities, spend time with God, and pray. Essentially, trust the process and stick with it, for it will yield the most beautiful results.

Prayer

God, thank you for your unconditional love that molds us as your children. Your guidance will lead to the most optimal life. Thank you for the perfect example we have in Jesus. For Jesus endured the cross and now sits on the right hand of God. I will trust the process despite the hurt and the shame because doing so will yield the most beautiful results. I believe this period of singleness is my divine development.

5.) WHOLENESS/SPIRITUAL RESTORATION

When God heals, he restores you back to the place He originally intended for you. He comes to make you whole physically, emotionally, mentally, and spiritually. Wholeness is a state of unbrokenness or undamaged. Trust the process of God making you whole, for he is the God of wholeness. Declare over your life, "God is able to heal me of all my brokenness. He is all powerful in the heaven and the earth."

Scriptures: "And ye are complete in him, which is the head of all principality and power:"-Colossians 2:10 KJV

Scriptures: "And the God of all grace, who called you to his eternal glory in Christ, after you have suffered a little while, will himself restore you and make you strong, firm and steadfast."
- 1 Peter 5:10 NIV

People are searching for wholeness that can only be fulfilled by God. Companionship does not complete you. It is devotion to God and yourself that makes you whole. You must trust God to bring you out of a state of brokenness. Some of you may be wondering how you would know you are trusting the process. What does healing and wholeness look like? At one time, God called me to lead a prayer group with my generation of family members. He awakened me with a few words: Arise, focus, trust, satisfaction.

Arise - Arise means to emerge, come to light. The term also indicates a spiritual awakening of who we are in Christ Jesus. He has given us all purpose on earth and a special calling. Arise in your identity in Christ Jesus.

Focus - Fixation on Christ unmerited salvation and endless devotion. It is all about Jesus. What you focus on reflects what is important to you. This is another area in which mindfulness will assist- becoming aware of your energy. The mind is a sponge. It will soak up the things you consume visually and aurally. The Bible instructs us to guard our heart. It is easy to say I am going to fix my thoughts on Jesus, but the application is key. You cannot listen to and watch everything. The Bible tells us to "Set your minds on things above, not on earthly things." (Colossians 3:2, NIV)

Trust - Trust that God is all knowing and knows what is best for us. We are His creation. Consider God's creation of the universe and how it operates as designed. We trust the earth will complete its rotation around the sun in a 24-hour period that provides day and night light. We trust the air we breathe has oxygen that will fuel our living. We trust the law of gravity which in layman's terms means what goes up must come down. Why do we struggle with trusting God and how he operates within us, his most prized creation?

Satisfaction - If you never had the companionship you desired, would you be satisfied in the Lord? Growing up, one of favorite songs to sing in the Junior Choir was "Happy". I recall screaming from the top of our lungs, "when God Spirit falls on you, makes you shout hallelujah. If you're happy, and you know it say amen. Happy in Jesus Christ." Our contentment should be of the Lord. I am reminded the Word of God instructs us to be childlike in receiving His Kingdom knowing our satisfaction is in the Lord!

In summary, when examining your state of wholeness, these words are relevant. If you are rising in your calling, focusing on Jesus, trusting his plan for your life, and your satisfaction is of the Lord, you are healed. Now as Jesus said, "Go in peace!"

CHAPTER FIVE
～ YOU ARE MY PEACE ～

Devotion to God, then yourself leads to healing. You need the Peace of God to maintain your healing. What is Peace? Peace is guaranteed assurance about the future. Synonyms for assurance are confidence and certainty. Since we are confident about our future, we can live every moment in the present. Chapter 4 of Philippians gives us perfect instructions on how to live a life of peace.

4 Rejoice in the Lord always: and again I say, Rejoice.
5 Let your moderation be known unto all men. The Lord is at hand.
6 Be careful for nothing; but in every thing by prayer and supplication with thanksgiving let your requests be made known unto God.
7 And the peace of God, which passeth all understanding, shall keep your hearts and minds through Christ Jesus.
8 Finally, brethren, whatsoever things are true, whatsoever things are honest, whatsoever things are just, whatsoever things are pure, whatsoever things are lovely, whatsoever things are of good report; if there be any virtue, and if there be any praise, think on these things.
9 Those things, which ye have both learned, and received, and heard, and seen in me, do: and the God of peace shall be with you.

10 But I rejoiced in the Lord greatly, that now at the last your care of me hath flourished again; wherein ye were also careful, but ye lacked opportunity.
11 Not that I speak in respect of want: for I have learned, in whatsoever state I am, therewith to be content.
12 I know both how to be abased, and I know how to abound: everywhere and in all things I am instructed both to be full and to be hungry, both to abound and to suffer need.
13 I can do all things through Christ which strengtheneth me.

These scriptures are indicative of a believer's thoughts, actions, attitudes, and overall perspective in life. In versus 8, God gives divine instructions on what to focus our attention on and how to occupy our minds. We must be mindful of what we meditate on and where our focus lies. Sometimes when our minds begin to wander aimlessly, we develop anxiety. Anxiety can be described as uncertainty about the future. It manifests in various ways including fear, lack of eating and sleeping. Let us not mention the somatic symptoms such as that empty feeling the in the pit of your stomach or the racing heart rate. Anxiety leaves us feeling hopeless which is why God instructs us to be anxious for nothing but everything in prayer and supplication. Then the peace of God which surpasses all understanding will be with you.

In versus 9, Paul instructs the church to do the things he has done. Paul heard directly from Jesus on the road to Damascus and followed his instructions. Therefore, we should also look to the Prince of Peace, Jesus, as our example. There was a popular phrase in the 90s, what would Jesus do? This is our motto as Christians for He is our perfect example. Jesus was concerned about the masses. Examples of His miracle working power included feeding the hungry, delivering those in mental and physical despair, encouraging people to take a leap of faith, and countless other marvelous works. Doing the things Jesus has commissioned us to do is literally taking on a life of peace. We should have a genuine concern for others expecting nothing in return. Most importantly, Jesus was totally reliant on God. He lived a life in total surrender to God's will and his purpose on earth. "Jesus saith unto them, My meat is to do the will of him that sent me, and to finish his work." (John 4:34, KJV) . He lived a life aimed to model the works of our Heavenly Father. We must do the same. In John 5:19, Jesus teaches, "Very truly I tell you, the Son can do nothing by himself; he can do only what he sees his Father doing, because whatever the Father does the Son also does." Having the mindset of Christ is our ultimate goal.

Versus 11 deals with our attitude. An attitude of gratitude regardless of your temporal state. 1 Thessalonians 5:18 reads "Give thanks in all circumstances; for this is God's will for you in Christ Jesus." Wake up with thanksgiving. Go to bed giving thanks. God led me to start my morning and end my day declaring three things I was thankful for. Develop a heart of gratitude. Focus on the goodness of the Lord and watch your life transform. We focus on giving thanks regardless of what state we are in because God always causes us to triumph. We should be a content knowing our future is fixed. This is our life's perspective as believers.

After God gives us the instructions, he affirms us in versus 13 that we can do all things through Christ who strengthens us. Wow, what a mighty God we serve. He knew we would experience fear and doubt, so He told us in advance we can do it. We can live a daily life of Peace!

Exercise

Peace is a daily practice and you must make that choice every day! The word of God instructs us to pursue peace. Ask God to instruct you how to develop daily habits of peace by following his instructions in Philippians the 4th chapter. Begin to record what God has revealed to you.

_____

_____

_____

_____

_____

_____

_____

_____

_____

_____

_____

During my period of divine development, I had to be delivered from anxiety. I learned two important lessons: it is critical to be mindful of what you meditate on and in every way chose peace! Our Father loves us unconditionally that he wants us to live the best life for His glory. God, the Creator of this universe, cares about everything that concerns us, and He is powerful to heal all manner of sickness and disease including our emotional wounds. However, if you continue to worry, it is indicative that you are struggling with unbelief. You can unintentionally bring the illness back upon you. Remember your thoughts are powerful and manifest into action. You need the peace of God to maintain your healing. Inner peace equals a happy life; inner peace is not dictated by outward circumstances, but by knowing and operating in the inheritance we received from the Prince of Peace.

Prayer

God, I need your help and divine intervention to strengthen, comfort, and give me peace. God, you are loving, and you care about everything that concerns me which is why I can cast all my cares upon you. I release to you all negative energy, distractions, negative self-image, low self-esteem, insecurities, doubt, fear, anxiety, rejection, and anything else that hinders my growth and development as a child of God. I bind the works of the enemy on every hand. Through Christ Jesus, I am set free from every demonic hindrance or attack. I declare my mind is regulated. You said in your Word, we shall have peace in you. I surrender Father. I cannot do it on my own. I need You, Lord. For you are my God, there no one like you. I love and appreciate you! You are my Creator, the beginning, and the end. The One who knows and sees all. I worship you Father, simply for who you are. Thank you, Jesus for the peace I have in you!

Scriptures:

"You will keep in perfect peace those whose minds are steadfast because they trust in you. Trust in the Lord forever, for the Lord, the Lord himself, is the Rock eternal."
-Isaiah 26:3-4 NIV

"I have told you these things, so that in me you may have peace. In this world you will have trouble. But take heart! I have overcome the world." - John 16:33 NIV

Chapter Six

≈ Finish ≈

I took me 11 years to fully break free of a relationship I knew in year one was not conducive to my walk with Christ. It reminds me of the children of Israel and how an 11-day journey turned into 40 years due to their disobedience. They had seen God's miracles firsthand, but still experienced doubt, fear, and uncertainty about what was to come. They complained about their circumstances and engaged in idolatry. Sounds familiar? Thanks be unto a God for second chances! Under the leadership of Joshua, the Children of Israel finished the task. They conquered Jericho and the land of Canaan. They received their promise. The redemptive story of the Children of Israel teaches us that God does not desire for his people to go in circles, going through the same struggles and repeating the same patterns. He wants us all to receive the "promise", but obedience is key. "The promise" in these times symbolizes our present spiritual inheritance. Healing, deliverance, salvation, and peace is our spiritual inheritance through Christ Jesus.

Although I was able to separate romantically from my former partner, we were still residing in the same household. I felt stuck and uncertain. I often questioned my purpose. What has God specifically designed me to accomplish? I believed I had the gift of teaching and God given ability to work with children. But in what capacity? I came across a word finish strong. Sometimes we feel stuck because we have not finished the task God has instructed us to do. We cannot fully grow in God if we do not obey him. Failure to put God first is disobedience. My aunt, Prophetess Kim, always says, "Hear God clearly and obey him quickly." When I examined every area of my life, I was at a standstill because I was operating in disobedience. I remained in the environment in which I experienced the stronghold. As a result, I still exhibited the same emotions, triggers, trauma reminders, and so forth. I was praying to God to fully deliver me from the situation, but on the other hand, I was doing things my way. One day I would feel numb and other days I felt overwhelmed with emotions. God wanted me to fully surrender it to him so He could give me the strength to finish the task.

In this case, "the task" refers to breaking free from relationship strongholds. Freedom from relationships that are not conducive to our walk with Christ. God revealed to me that I could not move forward in my full identity in Christ until I finished the relationship that was distracting me from my purpose. God will finish what he has started. He is a finisher!!! He achieves what he sets out to do. His promises are fulfilled through Christ Jesus. In John 4:34, Jesus said to them, "My food is to do what the One who sent me wants me to do [the will of the One who sent me] and to FINISH [complete]his work." From this scripture, the Holy Spirit showed me I would continue to have feelings of being stuck until I finished the task.

∼ Exercise ∽

Ask the Holy Spirit to show you what finishing the task looks like for you? What is God calling you to do? Have you been obedient to the voice of the Lord? Record your responses.

_____

_____

_____

_____

_____

_____

_____

_____

_____

_____

Scripture: "Being confident of this very thing, that he which hath begun a good work in you will perform it until the day of Jesus Christ:"-Philippians 1:6 KJV

THE GLORY OF THE LORD REVEALED

Hebrews the 12:2 reads, "[looking away from all that will distract us and] focusing our eyes on Jesus, who is the Author and Perfecter of faith [the first incentive for our belief and the One who brings our faith to maturity], who for the joy [of accomplishing the goal] set before Him endured the cross, disregarding the shame, and sat down at the right hand of the throne of God [revealing His deity, His authority, and the completion of His work]." With joy of finishing the work, Christ endured the cross and it now seated at the right hand of God. What could be more challenging then enduring the cross? We can finish our assignments with joy knowing our reward/ promise land is in enduring. God follows through on what he commits to. We are only experiencing a taste of God's blessings, but when we finish the task God has set before us, we will experience His glory. An abundance, an overflow, your inheritance and promises fulfilled. When we draw close to God, we experience freedom. Where the spirit of the Lord is, there is liberty!

Scripture:

"When Jesus therefore had received the vinegar, he said, It is finished: and he bowed his head, and gave up the ghost."- John 19:30 KJV

Poem - Freedom

I am no longer bound my negative distortions
I am free from self-doubt, the need to have the approval of men
I am validated by God.
My thoughts and words will align with the will of God.
For my desire is to please Him.
Lead me in your path and direction Lord

I am a representative of God which is why I must acknowledge Him in all my ways

In doing so, I am guaranteed victory

I visualize myself happy, successful, wealthy, spiritually, emotionally, mentally, and physically healthy

And until these things fully manifest in the temporal realm I will continue to meditate and declare these things over my life

God gave me power and authority to decree a thing and it shall be established

Because the greater One lives inside of me.

I feel empowered

I feel I can take on the world

Nothing can stop me

I feel reinvigorated, I feel freedom...

CHAPTER SEVEN

⤳ REST ⤳

You have done the work and finished the task. Your obedience to Christ will lead to supernatural rest. Matthew 11:28 reads, "Come to Me, all who are weary and heavily burdened [by religious rituals that provide no peace], and I will give you rest [refreshing your souls with salvation]. Take My yoke upon you and learn from Me [following Me as My disciple], for I am gentle and humble in heart, and YOU WILL FIND REST (renewal, blessed quiet) FOR YOUR SOULS. For My yoke is easy [to bear] and My burden is light."

Rest is a spiritual blessing. It is a period of refreshment and renewal. To find rest amid turmoil, requires taking on the yoke of Jesus. He will make all things easy to endure for the joy of His spirit lives inside of you. Rest also indicates continuous belief in God and His works. We give up control and trust that God Almighty knows what is best for us. Not only does he know what is best for us, He has our best interest in mind.

Scripture:

The Lord is my Shepard; I have all that I need. He lets me rest in green meadows; he leads be besides peaceful streams. – Psalms 23: 1-2, NLT

Prayer:

Jesus, I pray your spirit rest upon my heart. Help me to walk with you and allow you to take the lead. Help me to rest in the meadows of your pastures

We learn that Christ's way, is returning to Him as our first love and obedience. Allow devotion to God to take preeminence in your life. Come to God with a humble and repentant heart and allow him to remove any idol from our life. The more you devote your energy towards God, you experience his rest, renewal, and refreshing spirit.

I was able to rest in knowing God turned my pain into purpose. What I experienced is now a testimony to encourage others with God all things are possible. It is possible to heal from a breakup and mature in the Lord. Rest in knowing you are freed, healed, and delivered from relationship strongholds.

Scripture: "And by the seventh day God completed His work which He had done, and He rested (ceased) on the seventh day from all His work which He had done. So God blessed the seventh day and sanctified it [as His own, that is, set it apart as holy from other days], because in it He rested from all His work which He had created and done."- Genesis 2:2-3 AMP

Scripture: "So there remains a [full and complete] Sabbath rest for the people of God. For the one who has once entered His rest has also rested from [the weariness and pain of] his [human] labors, just as God rested from [those labors uniquely] His own."- Hebrews 4:9-10 AMP

We may have strayed away from our first love and sought validation from outside forces. Nevertheless, by the power of the Holy Spirit, we attained the mindset to walk in our spiritual healing. God was able to break us into pieces to restore us back into a beautiful masterpiece. This is Healing from a Breakup Christ's Way! Luke 22:31, details how Satan asked for permission to destroy us, but Jesus prayed for us that our faith may not fail. We have experienced our healing because Satan cannot not do anything except accept

God allow it. We are confident God has our best interest in mind. So, if God allows us to go through trials and tribulations, we know it will not destroy us. In addition, Jesus is interceding for us. The system is designed for us to win.

∼ Exercise ∼

The remainder of the verse instructs us to strengthen our brother after we have experienced victory. Continue to rest in God and encourage someone else that healing, peace, and freedom is possible through Christ Jesus. Brainstorm ways to share your testimony and spread the good news of Jesus Christ.

_____

_____

_____

_____

_____

_____

_____

_____

_____

_____

Additional Journal Pages

Additional Journal Pages

Additional Journal Pages

Additional Journal Pages

References:

1. Adams, J. (2013, April 19). What happens in the brain when we practise mindfulness? (Video File).
2. The Center For Anxiety and Mood Disorder's Trauma Institute (2018, September) What is Trauma? What is Trauma - The Center for Treatment of Anxiety and Mood Disorders (centerforanxietydisorders.com)
3. Davis, D. M., & Hayes, J. A. (2011). What Are the Benefits of Mindfulness? A Practice Review of Psychotherapy-Related Research. American Psychological Association Journal of Psychotherapy , 48 (2), 198-208
4. Kabat-Zinn, J. (2003). Mindfulness-based interventions in context: past, present, and future. Clinical psychology: Science and practice, 10(2), 144-156.

www.ingramcontent.com/pod-product-compliance
Lightning Source LLC
Chambersburg PA
CBHW071239090426
42736CB00014B/3146